Just a Miracle

Believing and Trusting in the Living God to work miracles in your life.

Book One.

Milkia Waller

JUST ANOTHER MIRACLE

JUST ANOTHER MIRACLE IS A BOOK ABOUT BELIEVING AND TRUSTING IN THE LIVING GOD TO WORK MIRACLES IN YOUR LIFE

MILKIA WALLER

DEDICATION

I want to dedicate this book to The Father, The Son and The Holy Spirit and to anyone that wants God to work a miracle in their life. In addition, I want to dedicate this book to my husband for his undeniable love for me, I love you. To my daughters who are my miracles and God manifested in flesh to me. Both of you have blessed me beyond words, I love you both. In addition, to my mom who gave me a mother's love, I love you mom. I also want to dedicate this book to my church families. Your love and encouragement has helped me in ways that words cannot explain and I am eternal grateful.

Table of Contents

INTRODUCTION

Just imagine being in that perfect place. That place of serenity. That place of love. That place of peace. That place of faith. That place where no devil in hell can take your joy. Yes, that place. All too often people dream of that place but never live to see that place. Is there such a place? Can you live a life in such a place day by day, hour by hour, moment by moment?

Maybe you say, "Yes, I can't wait to live there", or you may be saying there is such a place but it's not for me. Maybe you are thinking you have too many issues to be at that place. You may be saying once I get healed from this sickness I will be in a place of serenity, peace, love and/or joy. You may be saying when I get my dream job or career I will be in that place. Or perhaps when I get rich or have the financial stability, I've always dreamed of, I will be in that place. Or maybe when I have that baby that I've always wanted I will be in that place.

So many times, we are waiting on circumstances to change, some event to take place, something outside of ourselves to manifest in order to be in that place. But what if the change is you? What if the place is you? What is it about you that needs to change to be in that place? Is it a new way of thinking? Could it be that you are going through this so that you can bless someone else?

The Bible speaks of transformation of our mind by renewing it daily. But how can someone tell you about renewing your mind so that you can be in a place of joy, peace, love and serenity when you are in pain rather it be emotional pain or physical pain? I understand what you are dealing with I've been there. Can I tell you a secret? You will never win with a defeated attitude. You will never get better if you don't get in the place. You must transform your mind to begin to change and be healed.

9

As I am writing this book, I am reminded of some people battling cancer or fighting disease. They are in a fight for their lives and are in need of Just Another Miracle. I understand the seriousness of writing this book. There are woman suffering from a loss of a miscarriage and feel that their body has in some way turned on them and need Just Another Miracle. There are people dealing with a loss of a job, maybe by no fault of their own or even if it was by their fault, it is disheartening to lose a job rather you walk away, quit, are asked to resign or get fired, your income in some way is diminished and you will have to suffer financially with mental anguish of going without the income you once enjoyed which puts a strain on living.

You may have giving up hope and faith but know you are not alone and that God can and will work a miracle your life over and over again, if you follow the leading of the Holy Spirit that is within you. Smile, love, give and find ways to be thankful because God specializes in turning messes into miracles. I don't know you but Spirit knows all things and I am praying for your complete healing and transformation. I speak total healing mind, body and spirit.

Well I want to tell you a story of a person that began to live in that place. Someone that did not wait until circumstances and situations changed on the outside, someone that took life by the horns and began to walk it out, believing and trusting God. Someone who did not think of it as robbery to believe that being in this place, this peace of mind, would begin to work miracles in her life.

As I am sitting here at home, I am reminiscing on my life. I am wondering just how many blessings I have passed up. You see, my life has changed so drastically within 2 years and God has not withheld any good thing from me. I must say I am living the good life, the God kind of life, the Zoe life. This is the one time in my life I can truly say, "All is well in my world." Not because all the circumstances are great but because I have chosen freedom over everything. I'm very blessed today in my life as I spend time with my newborn and enjoy the new found freedom in having my own business, as well as the freedom to live my life the way I want. I wrote this story because I am a teacher at heart and I want to share want I learned within the past two years to bless someone. Maybe you can relate to what I have gone through and can use the information to live a better life or you know someone that have gone through what I have and if I can help someone by sharing or giving that is priceless. I believe that's why we are here to bless each other. When you put good out good comes back to you. It is my desire to see people living their best lives. I want you to walk in the miracle status that God has given you and I want you to know how to activate blessings in their life. I want you to get all that God has for you in this life. Think of me as a messenger from God.

Today, I am so grateful for grace, mercy, my life and accomplishments. My position has been changed by the blood of Jesus. I no longer let situations and circumstances control my life. I have peace, joy and I live by faith and not by sight. The by-product of this grace is that I am an owner of a successful makeup and cosmetics company that's called Milki Way Cosmetics & Skincare and a founder of Crystal Clear Children, a non-profit that is developing a generation by helping children to believe in God and themselves. I am a transformational speaker, who loves to inspire through God's written word and an author of, not just this book, but of a children's book called "ABC Faith" and a book called "Above Water." I have been married for a decade, have 4 children and I love my life. I have a Bachelor of Arts in Psychology, two Master degrees in Educational Leadership & Special Education, a Specialist in Curriculum & Instruction and I am a certified teacher and have worked in the public-school system for about a decade. In addition, I am a certified American Red Cross swim instructor, reflexologist and life coach. I am living comfortably; my body is physically fit; I feel good and I have the freedom to fulfill my dream of traveling world-wide. For this I am very thankful and I thank God for giving me everything I have.

But it wasn't always like this. There was a time when I was broken and did not believe in myself and I wasn't completely living in faith. I wasn't living with joy and peace. A time when I wasn't rooted and grounded in my faith. I let circumstances get inside my heart and mind and they made me feel like I was drowning in life. There was a time in my life when I was not living my life "Above Water" and at any time, if I took my eyes off God I would drown. That's when I made the decision to write my 1st book, "Above Water." I began to learn the spiritual principals to help me live my life on purpose. I learned from that place that I could live from another place. A place of freedom, of love, of peace, of joy and from this place, miracles happen. This is what I must share with you because I know you, I believe no matter what you are battling, you can overcome it. You can overcome that sickness, you can have that baby that you've been dreaming of, you can create the life you want and work a labor of love being financial fit. It's called purpose. God gave each one of us purpose. I believe no matter the circumstance, everyone is on a spiritual path, and I want to help you live producing miracles in your life daily but no miracle happens without first action. It was from this place of action, I learned that you can have what you want that is within God's divine will for your life in His timing. Yes, I said it. You can have what you want! God puts desires within our hearts, but it is our job to walk it out and live in a way that is pleasing in His sight, thereby obtaining His blessings and discovering your purpose for living.

This book will show you how God worked miracles in my life and how He can work miracles in yours too.

Consider this story. Steve Harvey said it best. "He said he learned it from Joel Osteen. Joel Osteen was telling a story where a man went to heaven and was walking with Peter. The corridor he was going down had a lot of doors and the man noticed that all of the doors had names on them. So, the man asked Peter what were the doors with the names on them. Peter responded by telling him not to worry about it and to just keep walking. Well they kept walking. The man messed around and saw a door with his name on it and he said, "Whoa, hey Peter, this door has my name on it. Is there something I need to know?" Peter said, "Don't worry about that, you are here now. Just go in there and talk to God". The man said, "No, I want to know what's behind the door". Peter said, are you sure you want to see what's behind the door?" The man said, "Yeah". So, Peter opened up the door. It had nothing but shelves in it, and on the shelves, were packages. All the packages had the man's name on them. The man asked Peter what was in all of the boxes. Then Peter replied, "Those are all the things that God wanted to ship to you. Number 1, you didn't ask Him for them, and number 2, you didn't believe you could have them, then you doubted Him, and then you felt like you weren't worthy." The moral of the story is that God only sends your blessings through FAITH street. I want all that God has for me and so should you.

Living Above Water was all about a faith walk for me. In that book I talked about the natural and spiritual laws of life, but in this book, "Just Another Miracle" I will explain the spiritual laws of life in more detail. I believe all the goodies in life go to the ones who believe. I believed that my life could change and it did. Suddenly while I was walking in faith Above Water miracles started happening and I would forever be changed. I began to focus on God and put my life in perspective. I had to learn to lean on the power within that leads me to my next step. I had to learn to surrender and submit to that power. Please read the testimony below and this will help put things in perspective.

MY TESTIMONY

At the age of 14, I was sitting in church listening to the preacher preach when he made an invitation to join the church. I got up out of my seat, crying all the way to the altar. I remember so vividly I was crying crocodile tears. They wouldn't stop flowing. I don't remember what he preached. All I remember is that I had a feeling or unction to get up.

God intervened in my life that day. At that time in my life, I had a great mother who worked hard to provide for me and gave me all the love that I deserved, but I didn't know my father and was searching. So, I joined the church that night but the church wasn't in me. I got baptized in the water. You know, dipped in the water. But when I got up, there was no real change. I still didn't know my father, and was searching to know more about him or to find him. Years later, totally living and operating in the flesh, I had a baby and my life changed forever. After I had the baby, reality set in, I thought, "Oh my God, having a baby is no joke". I felt it was the worst thing that could have happened. I was so ashamed, but Glory to God, it turns out that the baby was one of the best things that could have happened to me. God can take your mess and turn it to a miracle.

Okay, I had father issues and on top of that now I have a baby. I had to somehow make her proud that I was her mother. I wasn't exactly sure of what she should be proud of. I knew I needed God and kept going to church. I would later join another church. Again, I joined the church, but the church wasn't in me. I went to church, listened to a good sermon and went home with the same problems and insecurities.

You see, a real experience with God must not be confused with an experience with church. However, by this time, I was in college with no real direction. All I knew was that I wanted to be an RN because they had great salaries and loved helping people. So, I was on the fast track to get finished…you know the microwave generation where we want everything fast. Each attempt I made to rush through the process and make it happen if fell apart. I was trying to fix and make a life for my daughter and I but I never once stopped prayed about it and asked God for His help.

Now I had father issues, baby issues, single mother issues, college student issues and church issues. Even though I knew God was real, I was just a church member who had no relationship with God. I had that, "Oh will you help me" syndrome, like the man at the Pool of Bethesda. I was hungry for the Word and thirsty to find real men and women of God to teach me what I didn't know. Yes, I have been guilty of making people my gods and pouring all of myself into others so that they can say I'm okay. To tell me, "I see you". To tell me I still had worth. I learned very quickly that I couldn't look to them, because the words of people and the actions of people in the church are sometimes contrary. God is the only one who can fill your thirst.

But I kept going to church. Even though I continued to go to church, people still made me feel out of place. I just didn't fit in. At times, I would be up praising God, then the next thing I know after church someone would be cornering me saying I needed to wear a girdle because I was shaking everywhere. That didn't make me feel loved. It made me feel ashamed and self-conscious. But I never stopped going to church. Every time I received a Word I kept growing. The more I was filled with the Word, the more I recognized who God was. The more Word, the more I recognized who I was. The more Word, the more power I received. You see I learned I didn't have to fit in because I am a spirit living in this body. Spirits don't fit in.

Meanwhile, still on the fast-track, I had to finish nursing school. I was one semester away from graduating when I had a death in the family which was my cousin's Larina's mother. Anybody that knows me knows I love my cousin Larina. She has cerebral palsy. She has never walked or talked a day in her life, but the one place she loved was school. I went to school with her one day acting as her nurse and that changed my life. I made the decision to be a teacher. I switched careers and became a Special Education Teacher. In education, the more degrees you have, the more money you make. Knowing this, I went on to obtain 3 more degrees. I was learning to live on my own terms. I had a plan. I would teach for 10 years and then retire and do something else.

When I met my husband, I was a young lady on a mission. I had my own successful swimming business and had a career. I had learned a few things about how to be a lady and I had great women in my life which were my mom and grandmother. My mom taught me how to juggle life and how to be a go getter. My grandmother taught me how to be strong and be a wife. She had been married since the age of 18 years old. When I met my husband, we became very close, but had chosen to value each other, wait and do things God's way. So, my friend would later become my husband.

We got married with children from previous relationships. We had hopes of having more children but, after nearly 10 years of trying to conceive, nothing worked. I had a lot of failed pregnancies and many surgeries with extreme sickness during every pregnancy. I felt my body had turned on me. I remember visiting the doctor's office noticing all the women happy, smiling and glowing pregnant and I was holding a spit cup vomiting my guts out. I would literally vomit stomach acid and blood. But still, I was trying everything under the sun to have a baby. I underwent fertility treatments and artificial insemination and that didn't work either. It just wouldn't happen for me. So, I gave up and besides I was scared, who wants to be sick. So, I decided that I would venture out and fulfill some of my dreams. I began competing in pageants.

The world of pageantry opened-up so many doors. I wrote a book, started companies, began acting and modeling. I had access to places I never dreamt of. I was giving back to the community through summer camps, events, and mentoring. In addition, I had started going to another church. I began to get serious about my walk with God. I was learning about the Holy Spirit and its power and I was asking God for new levels with Him.

Essentially, I began to surrender. As for my career, I had a plan that I would work for 10 years and then retire and become an entrepreneur. I was at my 9.5 mark and then something happened, and everything fell apart. I lost the only father I have ever known (he wasn't my biological father but he loved me like his own) and I was asked to resign from my teaching job, all in the same week. I asked God, "Why me?" "What have I done?" "What sin have I committed?" This was devastating. To be honest, I was afraid. It's stressful to lose someone you love and not have a job. Initially, fear had gripped me. I had fear of losing what I had…my house, car, the businesses, my husband, because most marriages don't last when there are financial problems. My daughter was a senior in high school with a tuition. How would I send her to college? I started looking at my own humanity and death. I was at my breaking point. We all have something that has broken us in life. My security seemed to be stripped away. The spotlight seemed to be on me and I was afraid of the judgment of people. So, I had to ask myself, "Are you going to live your life for people, or for God?" I had to humble myself. The world that I had created was caving in. It felt like death. I had to get alone with God and after getting in the presence of God, I made a decision to choose faith instead of fear. I knew there was a lesson to be learned. Obedience to God will often mean giving up what makes us feel secure. I am reluctant to share but there is a certain amount of ownership we must take in order to be healed. And besides, I couldn't get mad at God because my plan didn't work out. Now I would surrender and ask God, "What do You want me to do?"

A couple of months went by, I was walking in faith and believing God and taking Him at His Word. I was good, and my family was good. I learned a great principle that God will supply all your needs according to His riches in glory. I learned that God was truly my source. God was supplying all of my needs and even gave me some wants. So, I still had to work and the Bible says if a man doesn't work a man doesn't eat. So, I began to pray and ask God what to do next. I mentioned that I had a business that I had started called Milki Way Cosmetics which was a makeup company. So on Mother's Day 2016, I decided to give away a gift basket of make-up. I had someone make the basket, and brought it to church to bless someone. Here I am, needing to make sales, but was prompted by the Holy Spirit to give out a gift basket containing my makeup. Sure enough being obedient, I brought the gift basket to church to bless someone. My mom won the gift basket and she gave it to someone else.

That same day I asked the preach if I could say something to the church. I was weeping and shaking, but still walking by faith, I told about all the miscarriages I had, and about how I endured fertility treatments, had surgeries, how I had been so sick that I had peripherally inserted central catheter (PICC) lines in my arm where my husband would have to connect me to IV nutrition each night. I shared how doctors had told me I may not be able to have another baby and my chances of getting and staying pregnant were slim. Then I spoke a word that scared even myself. I said, "I refuse to let my dreams that are within my reach miscarry, and I am going to have my baby". The church prayed. Then the service went on as usual. The preacher started preaching and then he stopped and said, "by this time next year Milkia you are going to have your baby." I received that confirmation with hope and gladness! What was so sweet about this day was the fact that my mom, husband and daughter were present. After that day I spoke no doubt. I believed I could get pregnant. I saw myself holding my baby. I did not try to force anything. I just went on as normal. I did not post it on Facebook. I don't remember talking about it afterward. But soon after, I woke up feeling nauseous and found out I was pregnant. I was so happy. I found out I was pregnant 4 months later. I learned it does not take long for God to work a miracle. Well, I had to believe again. I had to believe that I could carry this baby to full term. I had to believe that I would not get sick. I began to follow and surrender more to the Holy Spirit. I used this scripture, "Worship the Lord your God, and His blessing will be on your food and water. I will take away sickness from among you, and none will miscarry or be barren in your land. I will give you a full life span". I wasn't alone this time, I had the Holy Spirit and even though I had not joined the church, somehow the church had gotten into me. However, I would later join.

God is so good all the time, I was holding my baby on Mother's Day, 2017. God used Mother's Day to bless me. How ironic! God is so strategic and He can do anything but fail. What I thought was misery or a mess of losing a loved one and becoming financially dependent, God gave me miracles. I found my power and He showed me that He can do anything but fail. I learned that when the Spirit leads it is much easier to birth things in the natural. When I was trying to find meaning in a barren world (my barren world) and just as I needed more meaning, my baby was born. The system of this world is sinking sand but God's system is built on a rock, Jesus. When you hit the rock that's when miracles are born. God doesn't want us to hit rock bottom but if we do He is there to catch you when you fall. If you are experiencing any kind of loss know that you are just another miracle that God wants to perform and when the Holy Spirit leads us there's nothing we can't do. God is limitless and makes the impossible possible.

Through everything, I remember praising God through it all. I believed in His grace although I may not have been walking fully by faith in Him. I found my father, the Father and I know God was with me during every circumstance or situation but I had to learn how to live above water to get to just another miracle.

My oldest daughter that I had in my teenage years is my miracle as well. There is no way, I would be the person I am today without her. She has molded me in ways immeasurable. Statistics show that when you are born to a single parent, and a teenage parent at that, you also become a teenage parent. She has overcome and defeated that statistic and is doing well in life. This same daughter encouraged me along the way throughout my circumstances, helping me to see God. She would often say, "Momma, God's got you!" God gets the Glory for everything that has happened for me, to me, and through me.

JUST ANOTHER MIRACLE

If you just knew what I am about to share with you, you will be able to win over every obstacle, circumstances, or situation that you will encounter because winning is learning as well. I want to show you how I lived in the spirit realm and how I allowed God to work these miracles in my life. I shared that testimony because we overcome by our testimonies and because I thank God for turning my messes into miracles. It is not about me, but its all about Him and He can do the same for you!

Disclaimer: God blesses who He wishes and this book is not for you if you won't remove yourself from the naysayers. They must get out of your life. In the sections proceeding, I will help you loose things from your life and provide information to help in the process. All anyone can give you is information and what you do with the information is up to you. Let's begin to allow God to turn our mess into our miracle. I am going to share with you 5 spiritual truths, 5 is the number for grace, that will help you birth God's best for your life and allow God to birth miracles in your life. You are Just Another Miracle.

JUST ANOTHER MIRACLE

Genesis 1:26-27 Then God said, "Let us make man in our image, in our likeness and let them rule over the fish of the sea and the birds of the air, over the livestock, over all the earth, and over all the creatures that move along the ground."

So God created man in His image, in the image of God He created him, male and female He created them.

First of all you must believe you are a miracle. Yes, you are a miracle. Conception in itself is a miracle. What it takes to form a baby is a miracle. You are God's workmanship. He created you with something in mind. The mere fact that you are still here is a miracle. Every person on this planet is a miracle and has purpose. But how do we unlock our purpose, how do we unlock our miracles in our lives? I want to help you to see miracles in your life and live in a miraculous state of life, where you allow God to produce miracles in every area of your life, where you look for your miracles and expect miracles every day.   It's that simple, God works miracles every day. You see, miracles are God's way of telling you, He is still real and can do anything but fail. Surrender to God and the Holy Spirit within you and begin to obey.

Every time a child is born into this world, that's a miracle. What I have discovered is that everything is a miracle. Miracles are good. They are special and they are all around you. Miracles are love. The body you live in is a miracle.

Everything works interchangeably. I know you love your body that God created for you but consider for a moment that you are not that body. That you are indeed, like God, a spirit living in the body. If you are not your body, then who are you? Well the Bible tells us that we are spirit and that God made us in His image. So if God made us in His image then we know that God is a Spirit and not a body.

I want to let you know that in the spirit realm of living, you can have as many miracles as you want. You can learn to live in your body and have peace, overflowing joy, faith and life to the fullest. These are the Crowns of Life. You can have freedom, love, generosity, and a world class life of excellence. You can wake up every morning speaking life to yourself by saying I have peace.

I am joyful and I am living by faith in the true living God. The spirit is your God part of you. As a believer, you have God, The Holy Spirit living in side of you. When you accept Jesus as your personal savior, you have access to everything God died and rose to give you. He died for you so you can live. You are a miracle. He put something inside of you that is undeniable worthy. Believe that you a miracle are no matter what your circumstances look like. Because you are in God's image, you can rule and reign like God.

SEE IT

Faith is believing in something you don't see with your eyes. It is believing in a God you can't see and sometimes you can't feel. It's like believing in the air that you breathe. You can't see it but you know it's there because you breathe it and every now and then, you feel the coolness of the wind on your skin or you see the trees move. Having faith is believing in a God you can't see with your natural eye. Its believing in Him and knowing what you believe and why you believe what you believe.

Just like the wind is seen by the blowing of the trees, God will oftentimes leave evidence. He gives us signs and wonders and allows miracles to happen in our lives that are beyond explainable. The Bible records lots of miracles performed through God and Jesus. But it doesn't just stop at the Bible. God is still working miracles today.

Just Another Miracle is a book for believers. This book is for people who believe in the wondrous working power of Jesus. This book was written to let you know that God can still work miracles in your life and in lives of others. I have met countless people who God has healed from cancer, who have cancer but are walking miracles, given them children when the doctor told them it was impossible, and He has blessed them financially beyond their ability to comprehend.

All of the people made the decision to look beyond the sickness and see health, to look beyond infertility and see fertility, and to look beyond poverty and see wealth. Some decided that the job loss was just that, an opportunity for God to work a miracle and give them a labor of love. As I am writing this book, I am sitting in Barnes and Nobles reflecting on the rotation of the axis of the earth. I am reflecting on the way the earth rotates and the miracle of day and night. The miracle of season changes. NO man has the capability to make day and night and change seasons but God does. You may be in a night season but God specializes in turning night to day and changing seasons from gloomy to bright and it does not take long for Him. God is really waiting on us to see Him as our miracle worker.

Think on this: You are playing chess or checkers with someone that you love. Even though you love them you are playing the game for two reasons, that is to have fun and to win. Life is more than a game but along the way you want to have fun and win just like playing the game. We can say it is a game but you are in a fight. But the fight is fixed. I want you to know that if you walk in the Spirit you can never lose. Whenever you are in a fight there is always two opponents. The opponents are fear or faith. To fight God's way you must have complete confidence of what we hope for and the assurance about what we do not see. It is believing in God to take what man says is impossible and believe with full confidence that God's got you.

You see, Jesus has already won the battle for you, now you have to walk in it. You must see some things differently. You cannot produce the fruit of faith without being rooted and grounded in your belief in Jesus' finished work.

You must believe that God can make you new and have unmovable faith in Him. You must be able to stand still and see the salvation of the Lord. In my last book, "Above Water," I discussed the natural laws of life. In this book, "Just Another Miracle", I will discuss the spiritual laws of life. I started to apply them to my life when I had to depend on God to supply my needs. I tapped into the spiritual laws of life after complete surrendering to God. I began to try the spirit by the spirit. I began to work the principles in my life. The things I am sharing with you I have done and will continue to do. They work but you just have to work it.

Because I was depending on God for my income and had so many miscarriages, hyperemesis and surgeries, I had to learn how to believe God in a different way. I had to get serious and learn to walk in the spirit and walk in faith. So I began to strategize, I remember putting a beautiful picture of myself on my dresser mirror of myself before I became pregnant. It was a picture of me when I had financial blessings and was in complete healing. That picture helped me to stay focus and to see myself healed.

Spiritual laws are laws that are always in effect. They are always working even when you neglect to realize it. For example, my client was battling cancer and she was reluctant to tell her mom. When she told her mom that she had cancer, her mom immediately started crying and internalizing it. The mom told her daughter that she always wanted to out-live her children and said she wanted to die. It wasn't a year later that the daughter's mom passed away. The daughter is still living in faith with the diagnosis of cancer. She is doing well trusting God to bring her through.

Jesus Christ gives us a great illustration of this because He says whatsoever a man sows that is what he shall reap. Life is about whatever you put out in word and/or your own actions, they will come back to you. The Bible says, "Give and it shall be given to you pressed down shaken together and running over". Be not deceived. If you give out money, you will receive money. If you give out joy, love, and peace, you will receive these things. When you give out good, good will come back to you. If you give out discourse, you will receive hate and jealousy. Whatever you send out, you will definitely receive in return. The old folk have a saying, "It does not take long to get back what you give out".

In the Bible, Genesis 1:31, God saw all that He made, and it was very good. You have to know you are good to get good in your life. So, however you see yourself, who you see yourself to be and what you see yourself having, will manifest in your life. That's why it's so important to have a vision and make it plain. What your mind sees is what you will bring into existence in your life. So, have a vision that aligns with who the Holy Spirit says you are. This is how important it is to see yourself as being good: Like the mother I just spoke about. There was another woman I knew. This woman talked about having a disease. She often spoke about it and the picture became a reality in her life. That lady died a premature death because she manifested this in her body. She often spoke of having sickness and she even spoke that she would not live very long.

On the flip side, after having so many miscarriages, surgeries, and sickness associated with pregnancies, I never in a million years thought I would conceive, but I began seeing myself holding a baby and the next thing I knew I was pregnant after 10 years of trying, thousands of dollars spent and much grief and pain. I began to surrender to God and His way. His way is learning how to live in the spirit. I began to visualize even before I knew I was pregnant. I could see myself holding my baby. I could see myself healed and the results were favorable.

The Spirit within or the Holy Spirit has the blueprint for our lives. When you seek the kingdom first then all things will be added to you. But we still have a responsibility to train what we see and transform our own mind. Our mind is the part of us that must be transformed. Our power to rationalize can be a strength or weakness. Our mind is not spirit. Spirit knows who you are and what God has for you, but your mind must align with your spirit. When you start to train your mind, it may seem difficult to align your mind with your spirit. It's imperative to spend time in prayer and meditation so that you can weed out things that are not in alignment with your spirit. Your mind will play catch up with your spirit, that's why it must be transformed. Then, align your mind with what you saw in the prayer and meditation. This is transformation. It's important that you focus on what you see and what the spirit has shown you. By doing this, you will manifest good in your life. Your untransformed mind is constantly working from your past...your carnal mind or flesh. It doesn't know your future or your present, only the spirit knows that. The carnal mind can only see what is. It sees disaster, sickness, disease, pain, and evil. If you are constantly using the old faculties of the mind you will forever live like the old man. To be new, you must align your mind with spirit through prayer and meditation. Your inner spirit, often called the Holy Spirit knows all things. The Holy Spirit, I introduced to some in my testimony, or reintroduced to others, is ever present. It is one with the Father and the Son, but it is what Jesus died to give all believers. What I have learned is that when living by the Holy Spirit, you are living from the realm of perfection. Once you tap into the realm of the spirit you tap into your divine path. This divine path leads you to your unique path that God created for you before the foundation of the earth. Even in a night season, you will still be able to see.

I believe I was blocking the real path that God had for my life because I hadn't totally surrendered to the spirit realm of living. Once I learned how to see, my life changed in so many ways and God blessed me with a baby that I worked so hard in my flesh to get, and could not get. Something that money could not buy. Because it was my divine path to birth a baby, my world constructed everything needed to allow the birth to take place. You see, being asked to resign from the job was not easy, I wanted to fight for my job but didn't and although it didn't feel good, the process worked for me. God will fight your battle if you stand still and see the salvation of the Lord.

The book of James 1:6--- "But when he asks, he must believe and not doubt, because he who doubts is like a wave of the sea, blown and tossed by the wind."

James 2:14 "Faith without works is dead. Hebrew 11:6 Without Faith, it's impossible to please God."

Faith says yes when the doctor says no, it says yes when you don't see things working in your favor. Faith is taking God at His word. Anyone can live in fear. Fear is everywhere on television, in doctor's offices, in the banks, in our schools, our homes, and even in our churches. So, it is almost impossible to escape fear. The only place to escape fear is in our minds. There are a lot of people today that are proclaiming that they are believers of Christ which is great. But I want to ask you a question, do you believe in the world system more than you believe in the system of God? There are two systems. You see the world says when I get it then I will be. God says to be it or see it before you get it. Which system are you buying into?

For instance, if you are without and you are looking at a situation showing you that "without picture", if you only believe in what you see you cannot obtain anything different. You must get still and ask the Holy Spirit to show you His will for your life concerning that situation. Once you see it, ask for what you want, believe you have received it and act as if you already have what you asked for. See it and be it, before you have it then start preparing for what you have asked and received. Although the situation may not look favorable, your job is to prepare for success and God will bring His divine will in your life at the right timing.

In the Bible, there were three kings in the desert and they were without water for their men and horses. They consulted the Prophet Elisha who gave them this message: Thus, says the Lord, you shall not see wind or rain but make this valley full of ditches. You see Elisha told them to make ditches. He told them to prepare for the rain even though there was no water in sight. You must prepare for what you want even if you don't see it.

In another occurrence in the Bible, which is my favorite story in the Bible, a widower went to Elisha and told him that her husband, his servant, had died. She needed money to pay her debt. He asked her what was in her house. She said that her husband left a little oil there. Elisha told her to go borrow containers, lots of them, and go home and fill up the containers until she ran out of oil. And she did. When there were no more containers, the oil stopped. Then when she went back to him, he told her to go and sell the oil. The widowed woman obeyed and prepared for what she wanted. The number of jars she gathered was an indication of her faith.

God's provision was as large as her faith and willingness to obey. The Bible records that she had enough to pay her debt and some left over for her and her sons. In God's kingdom, there is a supply for every demand. In the world's system, there is a demand for every supply. We must be cautious of limiting God's blessings by lack of faith and obedience. God is able to do immeasurably more than we ask or imagine. With God or the Holy Spirit, we can win. Your carnal mind, the devil, or your conditioned mind will try to convince you that you will not get what you ask. But your power is seeing what is not there. It is in activation of your faith.

When you walk in faith surrendering to God to produce miracles in your life, you must realize that the blessing is that you can see even when you may be in a dark place in your life, if you are guided by the Holy Spirit. In the Bible, the twelve spies went out to scope the land and Caleb and Joshua were the only two that came back with a good report. All the other spies said that there were giants in the land. God can only give a person what you can see. If you can see it, you can be it. See through the eyes of faith.

I told you I lost the only father I had ever known and was asked to resign from my job all in one week. When you lose a loved one your body and mind become weak. I started questioning my life and started looking at my own humanity. I was so sad that I would never see my father again. But to top it off, that same week I lost my job. This was no ordinary job. I had invested all my time, energy and money into my career and the unexpected occurred. It seemed my life was dark. Initially, I had hit rock bottom in my mind. If I continued to feel sad there would have been a downward spiral in my life. I would have never come out of the situation. You see, faith gives you a ladder to come out of the hole. I knew in whom I believed and what I believed. I was more than a conqueror because I was not moved based on what I saw in the natural. It was what I saw in the spiritual realm. I began to activate my faith and initially I was thinking about the circumstances and situations that were happening, but, through the eyes of faith, I realized the situations were really happening FOR me. I began to walk in my position instead of my condition. I became empowered. The circumstances made me stronger and pushed me to my purpose. I had to have faith during what was happening, and now I am better for it.

I had people who helped me to see God in my mess. I had a friend who believed that I could conceive my blessing. She had a similar experience and had the paradigm shift or mindset to believe it could happen for me. People can help you birth blessings in your life because they are detached from the situation. They don't have the fear or doubt you may experience as they are not attached to what is happening in your life. So, when circumstances and situations look dim ask for help if you feel you are double-minded. God said, "If two or more agree about anything they ask for, it will be done for them by my Father in heaven". You can't fail if someone else sees you successful. If you find someone to believe in you and hold to the vision, it is more than likely to come to pass.

GIVE IT

There is something that only you can give that no one else can give. God created you, a miracle, with something divine that only you can give to this earth. But what will you give? How will you live your life to honor God? If Christ redeemed you from the curse of the law, then we owe it to God to live our lives in a way that is pleasing. We must begin to serve with a servant heart through our divine path for our life.

If you are having difficulties figuring out your divine path, your mind, when you are still, you will receive pictures or signals to tell you what the divine will or path is for your life. But if you are too busy striving for things that do not align with your divine assignment, oftentimes you will not recognize it.

For instance, in my testimony, I told you I struggled with trying to conceive for nearly 10 years. I told you that I was married and had children from previous relationships. I wanted nothing more than to have another baby. I had a lot going on. I didn't allow myself the time to receive so that I could conceive. There was certainly nothing wrong with wearing the many hats but I was giving in areas and was not giving much time to God.

After I began to spend time and surrender to God, God healed my body, I began to get aligned and transform my mind and a blessing came forth. Blessings can come forth for you too. God is no respecter of persons. What He makes happen for one He will do for another.

If you have experienced anything pertaining to a job, having trouble conceiving, or having difficulty in your finances, or has lost a family member, begin to surrender to God and begin to look for ways to spend time with God and He will show you areas where you can give. We don't give to get. We give in faith because that's what God tells us to do. It's about being obedient. I told you in my testimony that God had interrupted the church service on Mother's Day just for what he was planning to do in my life. So, on that Mother's Day, I was prompted by the Holy Spirit to give away that basket of makeup. **I gave**. I had to have faith to give a gift basket when I was just starting the business and didn't have much money coming in, but I was obedient. At the time, I wasn't thinking about myself, I was thinking about blessing a mother of Mother's Day. I wanted to get the name of the company out. I was not thinking about having a baby or even about my circumstance of not being able to conceive. I had given it to God and that situation was dead to me. I was good. Today, I know this to be true, whatever you give out will return to you but you must make the first move. I made the first move when I gave. I walked in obedience and something good manifested. Today I have a testimony all because I was obedient to the Holy Spirit's leading. What I learned was that for every demand, there is always a supply. When there is a need, our God will supply. All that is required of you is to give. Giving can be in a form of a question. John 16:23 Jesus says, my Father will give you whatever you ask in my name.

God is the source for all supply. The Bible says, I have never seen the righteous forsaken or his seed begging for bread. When you are in a circumstance where you have to start over again, you must begin to act with faith. See yourself as prosperous and act like you already have what you want. Put out or give what you want. Do not talk about poverty. That means that you must be in tune with the Holy Spirit, which is even higher than your intuition. When you are in tune and you give by asking, you will be guided as to the next steps to follow to receive. It is very important that you obey when you hear or get an unction or hunch to do something. Within that obedience comes your reward. If I had not listened to the Holy Spirit, today I may not have seen God's power work in my life. Everything may seem to be going wrong when really everything is going right. As one door shuts another door opens. What may seem like an injustice is a blessing in disguise. There really is no loss. When you take a spiritual stand, God will restore to you the years the locust has eaten. You will get plenty out of lack, injustice out of justice. This is the proof that God can and will work Just Another Miracle in your life.

I found so much value within my struggle. I learned how to activate the spiritual laws to live. I truly learned that God shall supply all our needs according to His riches and glory. I had to be without to realize that God can work a miracle in my life by using His ways. I am currently operating a successful make-up company and not only that, I am now getting paid for speaking engagements, writing books and coaching others to live a life on purpose. Remember it's one thing to say what you will do, but it takes courage to apply God's way to your life.

When you give your intention, and put it out there, you are basically asking God for what you want. You must ask and it shall be given, seek and you shall find, and knock and it shall be opened unto you. You can only be blessed through your desire, faith, or the spoken word. God's answer is always yes and amen. When you are clear on what you want, after you have spent time with the Holy Spirit, you can and will get what you want. God is the supreme power. There is no higher power. Fear has no power. I have said this several times for a reason, when Jesus rose, He rose with ALL POWER. Remember Jesus said, "Why are you fearful oh you of little faith?" Let God be God and every man a liar. Faith over fear is what is needed to align yourself with your divine will for your divine desires or assignment for your life. When you give worry, worry causes us to manifest things that are contrary to what we want. The Bible says, "You can't put old wine skins in new wine". Learn to give and create by getting aligned with the Spirit within and obeying what is being ordered by Him so you can receive your divine blessings or just another miracle.

So, when you help or give to someone you are truly helping yourself. You will receive only what you give. Your words and actions will come back to you one hundredfold. Whatever you sow you will reap.

SPEAK IT

Isaiah 55:10—"As the rain and the snow come down from heaven, and do not return to it without watering the earth and making it bud and flourish, so that it yields seed for the sower and bread for the eater, so shall my word be that goes out of my mouth: it shall not return unto me void, but it shall accomplish that which I please, and it shall prosper in the thing where to I sent it."

To obtain anything, you must activate your faith through your spoken word. Your words will not return unto you void. Your words and thoughts will manifest and create your world. When you send out and speak good vibes in the world nothing can stop you. Your words are your greatest asset. What you say truly matters. It matters to God, others and to yourself. It matters to people because what we tell others reflect our character and if we tell someone we are going to do something and don't, it's a poor reflection on us and the God that we represent. In addition, not keeping your word can make others to feel unworthy of love. It's very important to keep your own word because when you speak, things happen either for your good or your bad. It's imperative that you speak what you want and not want you don't want.

In my testimony, I shared with you that God sent a prophesy, a spoken word through me. I said, I am going to have my baby. As a Christian, I believe, I gave through my spoken word. When you speak your words, they will come to pass. Our words are powerful. Then a confirmation was sent by the preacher. By Mother's Day, I was holding my baby. You see I needed all of that to believe and God knows how to orchestrate events in your life to get you to the point of belief. I started seeing myself holding the baby. I had real expectation that it was going to happen. However, I did not try to force things to happen. I let God take the wheel. I was in total submission. I put God 1st. Although I had been through a lot of unsuccessful pregnancies, there was something different this time. What I didn't share in my testimony was after I had the baby I almost died. I ended up going back to the hospital and receiving five pints of blood. I had been speaking and quoting the scripture that said, "I will live a full life span." That's why I have to share this message with you. Don't ever give up on God. He can do anything but fail. What sometimes look bad or is meant for evil, God will turn it around and let it work in your favor. You see, because I sought the kingdom of God first, the kingdom that is within me, I believe the divine will for my life manifested. Your words can justify you or they can condemn you. "Life and death are in the power of the tongue and those that love them shall be filled".

Whether you believe it or not, your giving of your words has power. Speak your faith and speak it out boldly! You are a walking god. There is a lower case "g" for a reason. You are not the God who created the universe but you are the god that creates your universe. You see God has already done everything He needed to do. Jesus came, died, and was resurrected. But when He rose, He got up with all power. Jesus gave the power to believers and even told us that He died to give us a Comforter, The Holy Spirit. Now it's on you to believe in the Holy Spirit's power within you, to speak or give your word, see and give your vision to the world, and give time to God to transform your mind. Remember, faith without works is dead. You can speak yourself into a miracle of abundance or lack.

For example, I knew a man that hated his job, the supervisor, and just hated the entire atmosphere. He continually said, "I don't like these people and I don't like my job". He created a picture in his mind subconsciously of being without that job. Soon that man was fired from his place of employment. Your mind will create what you release. Say this with me, working is such a pleasure. We must begin to enjoy the work we do every day finding the miracle in every task, person and interaction.

There is power in your words. People don't know who you are, your capabilities or anything about you until you open your mouth. Your words can make or break you in the natural and in the spirit realm. When you know the power of the word, you will begin to watch and listen to what you say.

In the beginning God said and then it was so. Psalm 82:6 says, "You are gods, you are all children of the Most High." And you create your world through or by what you say, belief in what you say, and trusting that God can manifest.

When we speak good things in our lives; good things will happen. When you say what, you want and not what you don't want, your mind aligns with pictures of what you want and what God has in store for you. Often you will get some confirmation from a friend, book you are reading, or something inside you.

Our words are so powerful. We can use them to heal, prosper or to build each other up. It's kind of a catch 22, because when you don't build up and enrich others with your words, they can come back to haunt you. Whatever you say about another, you are saying it about yourself. For example, whatever I say to someone they will often say back to me. I called a grown woman "girlie" the other day and soon after someone else was calling me "girlie" as well. It returned to me very quickly. Whatever we put out, big or small, returns to us. I had to forgive myself for calling the other woman that, because when I was referred to as such, I didn't like it all that much.

I love the saying, "Change your thoughts, you change your words, change your words, you change your actions, change your actions, you change your results". Give it a try. Change your condition by changing your word. There is power in your speaking your words.

Every day I speak these things over my life and I believe you should to: I am blessed. I give thanks for this wonderful day. Miracle shall follow miracle today. Speak what you want. Make a demand for what you want.

LOVE IT

God is love. To receive God's love, we must spend time with Him. He has unconditional love that He wants you to receive. It is a love that cannot be earned. You cannot be holy or religious enough to receive this love. Certainly, you cannot do enough good works to get this love, all you have to do is receive it. When you receive His love you will receive healing for your body, mind and spirit. Know that no matter what has happened, God loves you. You can simply say, Lord I receive your love. Start to activate your faith by getting still quiet time listening to the Father. Love is your glory. It shines the light on darkness and nothing can harm you when you walk in the love that God gives. If you are in a difficult situation, God will tell you strategy. It may look like your situation is of defeat but God has you where you are for a reason.

You see, love is not an emotion. It is unconditional, always present and ever abounding. Love is a cosmic phenomenon. It opens up so much of life. Nothing happens without love. The joy of love is the joy of giving. Real love is unselfish. When you give love, you will receive love. Send out the agape love. See the divine God in each person you meet. Stay grateful for the things you have. God wants you to lack for nothing and live an abundant life. If money is considered more important than love, then that is greed. All disease and all unhappiness comes from lack of love. You must love. To manifest miracles, you must love yourself enough to forget those things that are behind and reach for what is before. When God is your love, joy, happiness and peace, you will see a difference in your life. Perfect love casts out fear.

Jealousy is the worst enemy of love. Bless people that do you harm. Face your feelings and release that negativity and love. I heard someone say that "No man is your enemy. No man is your friend. Every man is your teacher." I've learned that when you bless your enemy or negative situation you take away a reason for them to dislike you or cause you any harm.

The opposite of love is nonresistance. Nonresistance is "the practice or principle of not resisting authority, even when it is unjustly exercised". It is considered a form of principled nonviolence which rejects all physical violence, whether exercised on individual, group, state or international levels. Practitioners of nonresistance may refuse to retaliate against an opponent or offer any form of self - defense. When I was in my job situation, I could have retaliated or resisted, but I chose the route of non-resistance. I chose to remain humble. I believe if I had of resisted, I may not have had a baby.

Whatever you resist, persists. Resistance is a form of hell. It places a person in a state of torment. As long as you resist a situation it will be there with you. If you take flight or run, it will follow you and show up in another form. Surrender to the situation, or adverse situation and count it all joy. Declare it to be good and be unbothered by it to allow God to produce miracles in your life. The Bible says, submit yourselves therefore to God. Resist the devil, and he will flee from you. The only way to resist the devil is to submit to God first. We have to resist only by using God's power through the Holy Spirit which is faith, love, peace, and joy.

When you have disharmony or lack of love within yourself or your heart which is basically the seat of your emotions, you will release it into your world. You don't want to produce disharmony. Love, as if, you have never been hurt. Whenever a situation occurs in my life, failure or success, I say it is a miracle. Every failure can be transmitted into success. Even my failures are my miracles.

Love is change. It is accepting change for the people around you. We are always growing and transforming. Just think if you apply the spiritual laws to your life I have given you, you will undoubtedly start to walk in the person God has purposed you to be and change. You should not be denied love because you have changed.

A person must always feel good before things can change. Bad feelings produce a negative spiral which produces negative results in your life. Even though you are in a faith fight, fighting to love, don't make the battle yours. The battle is the Lord's. Your job is to love. Love the unlovable. You can't lose what God has purposed for your life when you walk in love. You can only delay your progress when you deny love in some form. You can't be pitiful and love yourself and others.

God is not a respecter of persons. If He did it for another person, He will certainly do it for you. It is your divine right to receive abundance. When you break down the barrier of resistance and lack in your own consciousness, nothing good will be withheld from you.

The opposite of resistance is love. Love despite of anything. Put Love first in all you are, do and becoming.

DO IT

Deuteronmy 8:18-" But remember the LORD your **God**, for it is he who **gives** you the ability **to** produce **wealth**, and so confirms his covenant, which he swore to your ancestors, as it is today."

If you don't take massive action and start living by seeing, speaking, giving and being obedient to God, you take a chance of living an ordinary life for the remainder of your time on earth. You can forfeit your peace, freedom, joy, abundance and love; all the things God promised you. You will live your life with more stress.

As human being, we are motivated by pain or pleasure. You don't have to live a life of pain on a continual basis for the rest of your life. I wish I had surrendered to God's way sooner, I would not have gone through so much emotional pain. You may be thinking that it's impossible to surrender to God, I was once in your spot. Trust me I can understand if right now you might feel that you can't implement this into your life. You may seem like on some days there is just no hope. Or you may say, I have a fear of being judged and being afraid it's not going to work out for me. I can understand if you are in that spot. But I lived this and I want to help you live by birthing miracles in every area of your life. I want you to be an overcomer. God makes the miracle happen, we just set the stage by surrendering ourselves to allow Him to move in our lives.

All disease has a mental correspondence. You must restore your mind when dealing with dis-ease because when you transform your mind you truly transform your world and put your body at ease. Dis-ease and lack comes from being without love. Remember, whatever you give you will get back. If you want healing, give healing in the form of love. In my experiences, I've learned even when bad situations happen, forgiveness is in order so that you can be at peace in the situation.

Once you forgive, you fulfill the law of love. All kinds of diseases are caused by a mind not being at ease. Un-forgiveness will harden hearts and has been known to affect the eyesight. Un-forgiveness is the trick of the enemy and your enemy may be the devil but power lies within you. For example, I forgive everyone and everything that I think has harmed me in anyway. I suddenly started to feel peace. If you feel peace within, you will certainly reflect peace into the world. God wants us to feel peace, joy and have faith in Him and prosper. He said in His word, prosper even as your soul prospers. I don't believe in prosperity; I believe in faith which is obedience to the still small voice within. It's important to remember that by your words you can rebuild your body or remold your affairs. It is very important to choose the right words. Your spoken words release the supply. The Holy Spirit will lead you some places you may think are unnatural, but obey. In my life, I have seen many miraculous things happen in every area of my life. So, trust me when I tell you that your power lies in what you don't see. You must begin to see what God sees for you and speak and believe it when all odds are against you.

The Bible says, the fear of the Lord is the beginning of wisdom and God sees you as perfect. It's time we see ourselves that way. Perfect in Him. We must get over our need to compare ourselves to others and enjoy the qualities and characteristics God gave us. Forgive yourself for not valuing and seeing yourself fearfully and wonderfully made.

And for the naysayers, God is in control. Vengeance is mine says the Lord. When you realize that all your actions have consequences and all your inactions have consequences, we will begin to take action for what we really want. "For every action, there is an equal and opposite reaction."

If only I knew how to activate faith street sooner I would have believed in God and took Him at His Word and would have begun to trust and surrender to His ways and will for my life. I know I would be a lot further with living on my purpose and would not had to endure most of the psychological pain I put myself through.

Spending time with the Holy Spirit, communing and talking to Him is wise, because the Holy Spirit gives us pictures of our divine destiny, our next steps of being in God's divine will. Remember, whatever you picture or see will be birthed. I had a friend who came to me with some health issues and we discussed speaking only what she wanted and what God said about healing. She created a vision board of seeing herself in perfect health. We prayed and I was prompted to give her a scripture. I gave her the scripture that God gave me during my pregnancy to hold on to which was, "Worship the Lord your God, and His blessing will be on your food and water. I will take away sickness from among you". (Exodus 23:25). We spoke healing and we discovered if she just forgave a couple of people and begin to activate her faith, she could have what God wanted for her. She came back to me healed with no more symptoms and expressed that she wished she had met me sooner. The glory goes to God! He is the one who births miracle. We just create the space for Him to move in our lives. So, it is important to know spiritual laws that govern the birth of miracles. When you obey what you see in the spirit realm, miracles happen.

Forgive yourself for not taking massive action to get what you want right now. Forgive yourself for not spending much time with the Holy Spirit, right now. We are all very guilty of not spending time alone talking to the Spirit within because we live in a busy society, but if we don't, we forfeit our destiny. Desire is a tremendous force and should be guided with precision because it can be destructive. If you force things into manifestation you can wreak havoc. You must relinquish personal will. Stand still and see the salvation of the Lord. Don't force your personal will on what you want to happen or on anyone else. The saying, "Let Go and Let God" comes into play because it is truly important to let God handle your situation. Give it to the one that can handle it totally. Forgive yourself from trying to force things into existence right now. Remember I told you I was trying to force becoming a Registered Nurse and nothing seemed to work. heck, I was even trying to force becoming pregnant and having a healthy pregnancy. God had a set timing for my blessing and He decided that He wanted to bless the church that day to let everyone there know that He was indeed real and is still in the miracle working business. However, I had come to a place of joy, peace, and faith and I had to surrender to God, and begin to walk in faith by being obedient to the Holy Spirit within to receive the miracle.

Its normal to feel lost, hurt and overwhelmed as you try to get a handle on what you should do after major events happen and often unexpected change occurs. But when you act from a position of faith, strength and knowledge, and not from your emotions, miracles happen.

For example, when faced with what your mind may call a negative situation, bless the situation and move on. Believe it or not where you are in your life is what you have attracted into your life. In order to move from where you are.. to where you want to go.. you must forgive. Forgiveness transcends.

Remember, your power lies in your ability to see what's not there; which is your faith. If you desire riches you must be rich in your mind. If you desire health, you must be healthy in your mind. Everything belongs to God and He wants to give you good things, even healing. "The earth is the Lord's and the fullness thereof". There is no lack with God. He has provided abundance for His children to enjoy. But the prerequisite is faith. You must stay on faith street to get to that place.

God often wants us to give. Gifts are investments. When I gave throughout my life, I believe that was the key that opened up the door to my miracles.

Think about this. Have you ever tried to save something for a rainy day? Well what you are doing is attracting that rainy day. Usually the money you saved will be used for a traffic ticket, someone may steal it, you may lose it, or some other occurrence that you didn't want to happen will undoubtedly happen. There is one thing for sure, we can't beat God's giving. Your belief is not in lack. It is in abundance. Your work is to believe in abundance. Walking by faith and not by sight, is not the easiest thing to do, but if you are going to please God there is no way around it. Keep going. "In due season you shall reap if you faint not." Jesus told us in the Bible to be of good cheer, and that He has overcome the world. People in the world always think in terms of lack, fear, and sickness. But people of the Spirit, think in terms of love, abundance, faith, and health.

It all boils down to this: when you know your own power, you must transform you mind. If you carry burdens, doubts, and fears, you are violating God's principles.

For example, when I said those words, "I am going to have my baby", I spoke my word and gave it to God and I was set free. I continued to be loving, harmonious and happy and I gave it to God. The picture I saw clearly was that of me holding my baby. What I could not see before, I saw this time because I gave it to God and did not think of it any more. I was no longer trying to make something happen. I had given up on all the surgeries and treatments and put my belief in God. I had the faith as small as a mustard seed. I still went to the doctors. I still took medicine for nausea to control the hyperemesis. Although, I was not on the medicine long. I took the doctor's advice and God's hand and walked faith out and birthed what seemed impossible. You can birth what may seem impossible to you. You are a miracle. Don't give up! Your next blessing is just around the corner.

STEPS YOU CAN TAKE TODAY

There are a couple of things you can do today. Don't give up hope! Forgive yourself and others. Know in whom you believe and know what you believe. Trust GOD and learn to surrender to His way. Block out a time to start spending time with God and begin listening to Him. After spending time, write down what you hear and begin to create a vision for your life. Begin to recognize the power of your words and speak faith, speak wealth, speak health, speak love to yourself and others. Feed your spirit with the word of God and positive things daily. Download my 21 days of Just Another Miracle affirmations on http://www.milkiawaller.com/ If you are a woman reading this book. You can visit my website: http://www.milkiwaycosmetics.com My prophetic lips lipstick/lip gloss line will empower you when you wear it to speak blessings instead of curses in your life.